MAIMONIDES

His Wisdom for Our Time

MAIMONIDES
His Wisdom for Our Time

Selected from His Twelfth-Century Classics

Edited, Newly Translated and with an Introduction by

GILBERT S. ROSENTHAL

A Sabra Book
FUNK AND WAGNALLS
New York

For Jonathan and Abby,
and for all the children of our time.
May their perplexities be resolved.

G. S. R.

Contents

Man and God   53

Sources   75

Introduction

I suppose that I am not untypical of my contemporaries of the 1940's and 50's. We were all in spiritual turmoil—the wake of the Second World War shook us profoundly.

Science and religion seemed antithetical then; religion was judged irrelevant. We were all hopelessly perplexed. Most of my classmates found their way in life in the sciences or in other fields of endeavor; I chose a different path to contentment.

But if the generation of the 40's and the 50's was in search, in doubt, in turmoil—how much more so the generation of the 60's and 70's.

Our world is in perpetual chaos; war seems to be our normal, daily fare.

America is strife-torn and shattered by internal discord; the crisis of racial tension seems far from solution.

The draft has disrupted millions of young lives; our young men are insecure, anxious.

We are witnesses to a sexual revolution; old standards have been discarded.

A new phenomenon—the drug culture—is convulsing young people; there seems to be no stemming the tide.

With it all, there is no happiness, no contentment, no fulfillment.

Young people are experiencing anomaly, hopeless alienation, deep-rooted frustration, and aimlessness. They feel lost in an impersonal, brutal world. *Malaise* pervades the atmosphere.

Some seek the answers in withdrawal from society—in the euphoria of "hippiedom" and pot and sex. Others find it in riotous involvement in society, in anti-social behavior, even in violence.

Does religion offer answers for today's young people? Can it be a gleaming beacon in the night for which so many are searching? Does the ancient religious tradition still hold answers for the challenge of our times?

Eight centuries ago, there arose a spiritual giant, a physician and scientist, who offered a *Guide for the Perplexed* of his day. His name was Moses Maimonides. And it was through his efforts that medieval Judaism met the challenge of science and philosophy —a challenge every bit as demanding then as is the spiritual crisis of our own times.

RABBI MOSES BEN MAIMON (Maimonides, or as he is popularly called in Jewish literature, Rambam) was born into a distinguished rabbinic family in Cordova, Spain, in 1135. The son of a well-known rabbi and physician, young Moses absorbed his rabbinic and medical training at his father's knee; his home was affluent and cultured.

In 1148, a fanatical sect of Moslems called the Almohades conquered Cordova and imposed a brutal choice on all Christians and Jews under their dominion: conversion to Islam or the sword. Many people fled the kingdom; others perished. The Maimon family was unable immediately to flee from Spain, and apparently feigned outward conversion to Islam—a fact that was to plague Maimonides in later life.

Meanwhile the brilliant young man produced his first book at the age of 16. It was a brief treatise on logic called *Milot Ha-Higayon* (Logical Terms).

In 1158, the Maimon family emigrated to Fez, in Morocco, where they remained until 1165. Maimonides continued his rabbinic and medical training in that cultural center. He also completed his significant *Commentary* on the Mishnah—a project that occupied him for ten years. It was published in Arabic when he was thirty-three and achieved for him wide acclaim. The introductions to the various tractates are still considered classics of style, learning, and logic.

Yet, the family could find no permanent haven. They moved from Morocco to the Holy Land, but the Latin Kingdom of Jerusalem was hardly a hospitable place for Jews, and in less than a year the family re-settled in Fustat, a suburb of Cairo. There, Jews were allowed to practice their religion without fear of persecution.

Moses Maimonides' younger brother, David, was willing to earn a living for the entire family so that Moses could concentrate on his studies. David became a jewel merchant and traveled extensively throughout the Orient and the Middle East.

On a journey in the Indian Ocean in 1174, David's ship was wrecked, and he was drowned. Moses was shattered by the event. His life now took a new turn as he was compelled to practice medicine in order to support not only himself but also David's bereaved family.

Oddly, the death of David Maimonides gave the world one of its great physicians and medical authors. Moses Maimonides' fame as a doctor spread quickly. He was appointed physician to the Grand Vizier, then to the Sultan Saladin, and to his son as well. Christian princes of the day sought his medical services. His practice was so heavy that he found little time for study or for rest.

As if his medical practice were not time-consuming enough, the Egyptian Jewish community chose him to be *Nagid*—their spiritual leader and spokesman, and representative at the Sultan's court.

Maimonides gained the esteem of rabbinic authorities in all parts of the world. Questions on religious and political matters were addressed to him from Yemen, Baghdad, Marseilles. Meanwhile, his literary output increased. He composed a compendium of the laws of the Palestinian Talmud, and a book on the commandments entitled *Sefer Ha-Mitzvot*. But his two greatest achievements were yet to come.

The first, and probably his *magnum opus*, was his *Code of Jewish Law*—the *Mishneh Torah*—a phenomenal achievement of lucidity, organization, and erudition. This fourteen-volume law book is a codification of the entire oral law of the Jews from the biblical era until the twelfth century. The work occupied the author for a decade (1166–76) and achieved almost immediate acceptance. The simple Hebrew made it readily comprehensible to students and laymen.

Maimonides' philosophical *magnum opus* was his *Guide for the Perplexed* which he wrote in Arabic purportedly around 1197, revising it constantly until his death.

The *Guide* was originally prepared as a series of answers to questions posed by his beloved disciple, Joseph ibn Aknin.

Aknin had led a rather unorthodox life. For a time, he lived as a Moslem, but ultimately he returned to his original Jewish faith. Nevertheless his doubts remained: science and religion seemed irreconcilable. Judaism and Greek philosophy appeared to him to be hopelessly incompatible. Aknin was a perplexed philosopher and yet a believing Jew.

It was in the hope of resolving these questions that Maimonides wrote his *Guide*—a treatise that became world-famous in his own lifetime.

Two Hebrew translations spread its teachings to the non-Arabic speaking Jewish masses; the *Guide* has since been translated into practically all of the Western languages.

Maimonides was a voluminous letter writer and the author of legal responsa. He wrote on a wide variety of subjects: resurrection, astrology, apostasy, charity, ethical conduct. His legal views are cited to this day.

Significantly, Maimonides was also a great medical writer, perhaps one of the greatest of medieval times. He composed his works in Arabic and dealt with numerous themes—asthma, fevers, sexual intercourse, psychology, medical ethics. He was one of the early practitioners of the psychological treatment of disease.

Thus, writing in his medical treatise, *The Preservation of Youth*, he noted:

Physicians have commanded that we beware of emotional changes in the patient and keep him under constant surveillance. We must also guard against emotional experiences that hurt the morale of the patient. In this way, the health of a normal person will improve—especially if the disease afflicts organs like the stomach or brain where emotional factors and melancholy play such a significant role.

In addition, Maimonides understood the significance of ecological and environmental factors in the prevention and treatment of illness.

In *The Preservation of Youth*, he wrote:

The quality of urban air compared to desert or forest air is like turgid, polluted water, compared to pure, filtered water. This is because the pollution of the cities, caused by residents, their waste, cadavers, cattle dung, and adulterated foods, fouls the air and creates malodorous stenches and noxious gases. It is best, therefore, to live in a city with an open horizon on the northeast, near high mountains with forestation and outside water. If you have no choice and must live near the city, try at least to live in a northeastern suburb, so that the northern wind and sun can dispel the air pollution and filter it as best as possible.

Of his family life we know little. His son Abraham inherited his virtues and bent for scholarship. He became *Nagid* after his father and carried on in the scholarly tradition of the family.

Maimonides died of overwork and fatigue in December, 1204. He was buried in Tiberias, and his grave in Israel is venerated until this day. The epitaph erected on his grave reads: "From Moses (the biblical leader) to Moses (Maimonides) there arose none like Moses."

What was the impact and the legacy of this giant of medieval Jewry? It was, and still is, enormous.

13

First and foremost, Maimonides dealt with the challenge of science to religion. He harmonized the Bible and Aristotle, he synthesized reason and revelation, and he doubtlessly saved countless "perplexed" Jews who wavered between faith and heresy.

"Accept the truth from whoever says it," Maimonides wrote. He never closed his mind or heart to any thinker, Christian, Jew, Moslem, or pagan. He devoured all of the philosophical and scientific works of his day. He incorporated the essence of their teachings into his *Guide*. "The gates of interpretation are never closed," he insisted.

His liberality of thought knew few bounds; his open-mindedness was unparalleled. He wrote that although he believed firmly that the universe was created by God from nothing (*creatio ex nihilo*), if the opposite could be proved scientifically, he would interpret the Bible to fit the scientific proof. His concept of God was new and revolutionary; it was in harmony with Jewish theology and yet in step with sophisticated philosophy.

By remaining a loyal and practicing Jew, and at the same time accepting the best of the Graeco-Moslem philosophical world, he showed that faith and reason need not be inimical. This great synthesis inspired Jews, Christians, and Moslems. Thomas Aquinas acknowledged his debt to Maimonides, as did Albertus Magnus. Even critical philosophers like Leibnitz and Spinoza drew much from Maimonides' teaching.

In addition, Maimonides introduced a historical-critical spirit into the study of religion. He mastered comparative religion and anthropology and developed a modern's understanding of religious institutions.

For example, when he analyzed the development of animal sacrifices among Jews, he noted that God could not possibly have weaned Israel away from *all* sacrifices in one fell swoop. Instead, He had to proceed gradually, first, by abolishing human sacrifice through the substitution of animal offerings, then by replacing Temple sacrifices with the purely spiritual and intellectual worship of God.

Maimonides' analysis of Jewish practices is extraordinary; it reveals his deep insight into pagan cultures. His thesis was that every Jewish rite has some rational or historical motivation—although that motivation may temporarily elude us. He was convinced that many biblical commandments were meant to sever Judaism from its pagan antecedents.

In short, in his approach to religion, Maimonides anticipated much of modern religious thinking. He was centuries ahead of his time.

Finally, Maimonides helped make the "oral Torah" the legacy of all. The Talmud has always been an abstruse and esoteric subject. Only dedicated scholars can master it. But Maimonides gave the "oral Law" to the world. His *Mishneh Torah* (*Code of the Law*) is a model of lucidity and learning, simplicity and scholarship. Maimonides was not exaggerating when he suggested that the average student would henceforth have to study only the Bible and his *Code* in order to know Jewish law.

Although Maimonides was a man of peace, avoiding controversy and admonishing his students not to respond harshly to critics, he could not avoid controversy in his lifetime nor after his death.

Many scholars chided him for his failure to list sources in the *Mishneh Torah*. Others feared that his work would obviate the study of the Talmud.

But the greatest criticism was leveled at his *Guide*. The reactionaries and super-pietists labeled it a heretical work. In 1230, a group of purists even succeeded in persuading the Church to burn the *Guide*—an act that was soon to boomerang to the dismay of all European Jewry. Pro-Maimonideans battled anti-Maimonideans for almost a century. Some sages even banned the *Guide* to all but mature Talmudists.

Yet, with it all, Maimonides achieved immortality and his critics were consigned to the footnotes of history. For none of his detractors was able to bridge the two worlds of religion and reason as brilliantly as he had.

In a sense, Maimonides laid the foundation for modern religious

15

scholarship and philosophy. Although it is true that much of his philosophical and scientific system is medieval, his legacy is still fresh and vital. He showed the "perplexed" that one can be a man of science and religion at the same time; that reason and revelation need not be inimical; that one can serve God and truth without compromising one or the other, by no means a minor achievement.

For the perplexed and the confused of our time, the universality, humanism and depth of insight of Maimonides have special meaning.

If even one reader of this volume of Maimonides' views on the good life will find a new path to a happier, more rewarding, more fulfilling life—then the effort of compiling this material will have been amply rewarded.

G.S.R.

I

Man and Himself

Silence and Speech

I have discovered no better trait than silence.

What a wise observation! For inevitably, the more words one utters, the more one sins against some human being. And the fewer the words, the less the chances for sin.

Of course, there are various categories of speech. Some speech is purely damaging and devoid of any utility; some is partly damaging and partly careful; some is totally innocuous; some is totally useful.

I prefer to divide human speech into five categories.

The first category consists of sacred speech which God commands us. By this I mean the study of Bible, prayer, and any other verbal activities favored by Scripture.

The second is speech forbidden to us by the Bible such as false witness, lies, gossip, curses, obscenities, and slander. Slander is particularly evil: it destroys the slanderer, the listener, and the victim alike.

The third type is common speech which is neither useful nor sinful. By this I mean the normal, daily, and idle talk common to most humans. Pious people try to diminish such idle chatter.

The fourth is most desirable. It includes speech designed to exalt intellectual faculties and ethical qualities while denigrating intellectual and ethical defects. Through the techniques of stories and poems, such speech attempts to develop ethical behavior in people. It warns the listener to shun character defects; it praises virtuous people and lauds their ways so as to stir the listener to emulate their example.

The fifth category of speech is practical talk—speech connected with a person's business activities, food, drink, clothing, and other daily necessities. Such speech is morally neutral; it is neither virtuous nor evil. Nevertheless, it is best to keep such talk at a minimum. The ethical man abstains totally from prohibited or sinful talk, and he speaks but little of mundane matters. On the other hand, he speaks of divine and intellectual matters all the days of his life.

But two warnings are in order.

First, a man's deeds should harmonize with his words. Let him practice what he preaches.

Second, let a man say little and do much. Better to be a person of action rather than words.

★ ★ ★

Man's Quest: Intellectual Achievement

What is man's singular function here on earth?

It is, simply, to contemplate abstract intellectual matters and to discover truth.

Surely it is absurd to argue that man's purpose on earth is merely to eat and drink and copulate, or to build a palace, or become a king.

These are merely incidental functions, and they do not add to his inner powers.

It is *wisdom* that adds to man's inner powers and raises him above the crassness of life into the honored realm. He fulfills his human potential through wisdom; he rises above the animal within himself, because logic and intellect are what distinguish between man and beast.

And the highest intellectual contemplation that man can

develop is the knowledge of God and His unity. All other wisdom is merely auxiliary to this central truth.

In sum, the purpose of man in this world is to be *wise* and *good*.

If this is so, you ask, then why has God put ordinary people on earth who are incapable of abstract, intellectual thought? They obviously form the majority of humanity: the intellectuals comprise but a small minority.

There are two answers to this question:

First, the non-intellectuals are here on earth to serve the few intellectuals and to perform vital services. For if everyone engaged in spiritual and philosophical pursuits, then the order of society would be disrupted and humanity would quickly disappear.

After all, man needs material things, too. And someone has to do all the plowing and reaping, the threshing and baking, the building and carpentry, the sewing and weaving. The intellectual has enough trouble developing his mind; he cannot be expected to perform these duties as well.

Second, the intellectuals will always form a small minority of society. This is, apparently, God's will. But man is basically a social creature: he needs a society, he cannot be isolated. Consequently, God created the masses to form the society in which wise men make their homes lest they be lonesome and desolate.

★ ★ ★

The Greater The Man, The Greater His Drives

I have examined the teachings of our sages concerning the matter of man's corrupt drives and instincts. And I have concluded that they believe that better is the man who does crave certain sins and possesses corrupt drives than he who never craves anything evil and is content to ignore his passions entirely.

In fact, the sages have actually taught that the greater the man, the greater his passions and his regrets in avoiding temptation.

★   ★   ★

Poor Habits and Bad Education

There are certain concepts which the human mind can conceive by virtue of its nature and capacity. On the other hand, there are other concepts which our minds cannot conceive because of our limited intellectual and conceptual capacities.

Let me offer a simple analogy: A man can lift two hundred pounds, but he surely cannot lift a ton! Some men may be physically able to lift more than others. But there is a limit to every man's physical strength. Similarly, there is a limit to every man's mental capacity: the human intellect has limits beyond which it cannot go.

There is little confusion of ideas in the exact sciences or natural science. But a great deal of confusion exists in religious and spiritual matters.

According to Alexander of Aphrodisias, there are three causes of these differences of opinion. The first is man's lust for power and prestige. The second is the subtlety and profundity of the subject studied. The third is the obtuseness of the man seeking after the truth. All three factors lead man astray from perceiving truth, writes Alexander.

In my opinion, there now exists a fourth source of intellectual error—a source that did not exist in his days. That fourth source of error is habit and education. Men naturally love the things to which they are accustomed; they are inclined towards customs with which they are most familiar. For example, country folk prefer their rustic village lives—with all the inconveniences and primitive facilities—to all of the luxuries of city life.

Similarly, men prefer the opinions to which they are accustomed and in which they have been brought up: they love them, they defend them and they scorn other views. For this reason, then, many people fail to perceive the truth in spiritual matters, and they cling to errors such as anthropomorphisms and other baseless notions.

★ ★ ★

Limits to Human Intellect

Just as there is a limit to the use of man's physical powers, so is there a limit to the use of his intellectual powers. Too much speculation and scientific investigation can exhaust a man's intellect and lead to doubt and confusion. Sometimes it is good to admit doubt and acknowledge that not everything can be absolutely proved. If you come to this point of development, you have reached the pinnacle of human perfection and you are on a par with Rabbi Akivah who "entered the study of metaphysics and emerged from it unscathed."

But if you reach beyond human comprehension or deny matters that have never been truly disproved, or which are, in fact, remotely possible, then you might end up like Elisha ben Abuya, the heretic—confused, imperfect, skeptical, and flawed.

But do not think that our Prophets and sages were trying to shut the gate of speculation or destroy man's intellectual quest for attainable truths, as is maintained by some fools who make a virtue of their ignorance and belittle the wisdom of others and accuse others of heresy.

I have merely sought to point out that the Prophets and sages were correct in trying to show us that there are limits to the human intellect.

★ ★ ★

A Purpose to the Universe

In my view, the Bible and philosophical teachings seek to convince us that we must not believe that everything in this universe has been created for man. On the contrary, all things were created for their own sake, not for the sake of anything else.

I subscribe to the view that the universe was created at a specific point in history. I also believe that God created all items in this universe—some for their own sake, some for the sake of others. Just as God willed the existence of the human species, so did He will the existence of the heavens and stars and angels. But I am firm in my view that the universe was created by God's will—and we need not seek a purpose or reason, for we will only end up confused by such a quest. It is enough for man to accept the view that we are here because of Divine Will—or, if you prefer, Divine Wisdom.

★ ★ ★

Develop a Moral Character

It is important to realize that moral virtues and defects are only implanted in man's soul and character by exercise, constant repetition, and frequent application. If such activities and exercises are good, then virtue accrues to man; if, however, they are evil, then the result is moral corruption.

Since man is neither virtuous nor defective from birth, man becomes accustomed to the moral or immoral way of life from his childhood, depending upon his environment, his associations, and the practices of his relatives and colleagues.

Consequently, a person must constantly work towards moral perfection and strive to attain moderate character traits —always avoiding extremes, except in order to cure an evil extreme. The perfect man must constantly reflect on his moral condition; he must weigh his actions and scrutinize his spiritual qualities every day.

If he notices himself slipping into some vice, let him hasten to apply the remedy and not allow vice to become strong and implanted in him by repetition. Likewise, he should set his defects before him as a constant reminder of the need for self-improvement and spiritual healing. For, as I have noted, there is no man without some failings.

When a person weighs his actions carefully and constantly seeks to improve his actions, then he rises to the highest human level. He approaches God and perceives His goodness —and this is the perfect way of Divine worship.

★   ★   ★

Mercy, Justice, Righteousness

Ancient and modern philosophers have shown that there are four types of perfection towards which man strives.

The first and basest form is the one towards which most men struggle all their days—namely, the perfection of wealth through the acquisition of money, clothing, jewels, slaves, land, and the like.

The second type relates to the human body—it is the perfection of man's physique, the attainment of an even disposition, bodily strength and the like. Clearly this is not the highest perfection, since the drive for physical perfection is a sensual matter and differs little from the drive of an animal for health.

The third type of perfection is more uniquely human. It is moral perfection—the attainment of the highest ethical development. Most of the commandments of Judaism attempt to develop this kind of perfection. But even this type of perfection is not the highest; it is merely preparation for the highest type of human perfection.

The fourth kind of perfection in man is truly the highest. It is the attainment of rational values. By this I mean the conception of ideas that will lead to true knowledge of God. This is the highest achievement of man; it is his ultimate perfection. Through it, he attains immortality and human fulfillment.

The Prophets have taught us this matter in the same way as the philosophers. They have explicitly explained that total perfection comes not from possessions, not from bodily health, not from virtuous living—but from the knowledge of God, for that is the only perfection in which one can glory and which one should desire. As Jeremiah declared: "Thus said the Lord, Let not the wise man glory in his wisdom, neither let the mighty man glory in his might, let not the rich man glory in his riches; but let him that glories glory in this, that he understand and know Me, that I am the Lord who exercise mercy, justice, and righteousness in the earth; for in these things I delight."

This verse clearly shows us that the actions of God which one must know and emulate are mercy, justice, and righteousness. And note that the Prophet adds another important idea—

one that is perhaps fundamental to the Torah—namely, the phrase, "in the earth." God's providence extends to the earth, according to its needs, even as it extends to heaven, according to its needs.

My purpose in explaining the verses in Jeremiah was to show that man's fullest perfection in which he can truly glory is in achieving, to the best of his ability, a comprehension of God, an understanding of His providence over His creatures, and a knowledge of how He conducts the affairs of the world. Then man can imitate God and become God-like by leading a life of mercy, justice, and righteousness.

★ ★ ★

Business Dealings

A scholar must be honest in all his business dealings. When he says "No" he means "No" and when he says "Yes" he means "Yes." He is careful to calculate honestly. He pays his bills promptly. He sticks to his promises and never breaches an agreement. He never encroaches on someone else's business and he never mistreats anyone. In short, he prefers to be among the persecuted rather than the persecutors and among the offended rather than the offenders.

★ ★ ★

Lust and Sensuality

It is the purpose of Torah to make man reject and despise lust and to diminish his appetites as best as possible. He should indulge in his sensual drives only when necessary. It is well-known that intemperance in eating, drinking, and copulation destroys man's perfection and is injurious to him.

Moreover, overindulgence in such activities upsets the social order and disturbs domestic relations. When one follows his passions in the manner of fools, he neglects and damages his intellect and body; he dies before his time and causes anguish and worries to increase. He also multiplies the amount of envy, hatred, and wars in the world, for sensual men will do anything to take things from other men to satisfy their lusts, since that is the highest goal of their lives.

God in His wisdom has therefore given us commandments to counteract this goal in life and divert our attention from such activities. He has also sought to bar us from anything that leads us merely to lust and sensual pleasure.

★   ★   ★

Moral and Intellectual Goals

It is not enough for man to be a mere pragmatist or to strive to attain physical health and freedom from disease alone. Such a person is surely no saint.

Physical and sensual satisfaction is not, *per se*, the true goal of man's actions. The proper goal for man is this: Let him strive for physical health so that his body and limbs might be perfect and his soul can attain moral and intellectual eminence without the hindrance of a sick body.

Likewise, let a man master sciences and philosophy and practical skills—mathematics, draftsmanship, technology, engineering, mechanics, and what have you—in order to sharpen his intellect and improve his logical faculties so as to attain the true knowledge of God's existence.

★   ★   ★

Asceticism Is an Evil Road

Perhaps you might argue: "Since envy and lust and similar traits are evil and shorten a man's life, I will separate totally from them and go to the opposite extreme. I will not eat meat or drink wine; I will not marry or live in a fine home; nor will I wear good clothing but, instead, I will don sackcloth and coarse wool like the Christian monks."

I say that this is an evil road to follow. It is prohibited to take this path. And the man who follows this path is a sinner. Consequently, the sages commanded man not to deny himself any pleasures except those denied him by the Torah. Nor should a person heap oaths and vows of abstinence and denial on himself.

Those who are accustomed to fast frequently are not walking the best road. For the sages have prohibited a man from afflicting himself with constant fasting. Concerning these and similar excesses, King Solomon admonished: "Do not be overly righteous nor overly wise lest you come to grief."

★　★　★

Sensuality and the Good Life

Man's sins and shortcomings originate in the substance of the body but not in its form. Thus, the knowledge of God, the formation of ideas, the mastery of lusts and passions, the ability to distinguish between that which is to be chosen or rejected—all of these qualities are due to man's form.

But eating, drinking, sexual relations, and most of man's lusts and passions as well as all of his vices originate in his substance or matter. Of course, there are different types of men who approach the problem of sensuality differently.

Some persons constantly strive to choose the noble way of life. They do not cater to their human substance or their bodies; but they cultivate their forms, that is, they utilize their intellects, they cultivate ideas, they strive to achieve true knowledge of everything, and they seek communion with the Divine Intellect which emanates to man and which is the source of human form.

When the needs of their bodies or their lustful drives lead them to base doings, they grieve and sense shame and remorse. Consequently, they endeavor to diminish this disgrace with all their might and they struggle to guard against it in every possible way.

There are human beings who go to extremes in curbing sensuality. They consider all sensuality disgraceful and shameful. They single out for special condemnation the sense of touch, for as Aristotle notes, that sense is the cause of our desire for food, drink, and sex.

My view is that the intelligent man must reduce his sensual wants and drives as much as possible. He must feel somewhat guilty when satisfying them; he must never speak of them, nor publicly indulge in them in the company of others. Man must rule over these passions and appetites so as to curb them as best as possible. He must satisfy them only to fill his needs. His purpose in life must be the purpose of man as a human being: he must formulate ideas and nothing else. And the most powerful of these ideas is the conception of God and His creation and deeds. Man must ponder these concepts to the best of his ability. Such a man is constantly with God.

Conversely, those fools who neglect intellectual pursuits and only cultivate sensual pleasures and set as their goal in life the indulgence of their appetites, are separated from God.

When a man possesses a good body and normal sensual drives that do not overwhelm him and do not upset the order of his life, he has truly a Divine gift. In short, a good constitution implies that man's soul can rule over the body. And even if this is not so in a particular case, a person can train himself to conquer his lusts and appetites. This in fact is the purpose of the laws of the Bible.

★ ★ ★

The Hebrew Language and Sex

In my opinion, one should not speak loosely about sexual intercourse, nor should one's thoughts be preoccupied with such matters. But above all, one must never discuss such matters in a lewd or obscene way.

Since speech is a unique attribute of man and a special gift of God to distinguish him from other creatures, it must be used for human perfection, to learn and to teach, but never for degrading or lewd purposes.

I have good reason for calling Hebrew the holy tongue. Do not think that I am exaggerating or in error in this matter. The proof is simply this: Hebrew has no special names for the genital organs, neither for male nor female, nor does it have any explicit terms for copulation, semen, or ova. All of these terms are described by euphemisms or metaphors or allusions.

The point is clear: we should be chaste and discreet about such matters. And if we must discuss them, then we should do so modestly by using euphemisms and metaphors.

★ ★ ★

Friendship, Prostitutes, Chastity

It is well-known that man requires friends all of his life, as Aristotle has explained in the ninth book of his *Ethics*. When healthy and successful, man enjoys company. When in trouble, he certainly needs friends. And when old and sick — he is aided by friends.

This type of love is more intense between parents and children, and it is also prevalent among close relatives. Perfect love, brotherhood, and mutual help are found only among close relatives. Clans descended from common ancestors exhibit a certain feeling towards one another — a feeling of love, of mutual help, of pity and compassion. And one of the chief purposes of the Torah was to foster these qualities in men.

For this reason, the Torah outlawed prostitution. The teachers of our faith believed that prostitution destroys family relationships. Moreover, illegitimacy results, and there is no more horrible situation than one in which a child does not know his parents or family. The prohibition also seeks to curb excessive lust and sexuality, and the strife that results from men competing for the favors of harlots. Consequently, sexual intercourse is only permitted when a man has chosen a specific woman as his wife and marries her publicly.

Otherwise, most men would bring harlots to their homes and live with them as husband and wife. In order to prevent this profanation of the marital union, Jewish tradition commanded us to choose a wife formally by the act of betrothal, and then marry her in a public ceremony.

The laws prohibiting consanguinity, incest, pederasty, homosexuality, and zoophilia seek to teach us that sexual intercourse is to be limited, disdained, and kept at a minimum. If natural intercourse is disdained as a necessary biological act, how much more so are aberrations whose performance is unnatural and whose sole purpose is pleasure. Another reason for these prohibitions is to inculcate chastity in our hearts.

★ ★ ★

Marriage: A Public Ceremony

Before the Torah was given, a man might covet a woman whom he chanced upon in the market place. If both agreed, he could then take her to his house and have sexual relations with her, and she might become his wife without any formal public act. After the Torah was given, however, the Israelites were commanded that if a man desires a woman, he must first acquire her in the presence of witnesses, and then he may take her as his wife.

The reason for the prohibition against harlotry is clearly stated in the Torah: "Do not degrade your daughter, by making her a harlot, lest the land fall in harlotry and be filled with depravity."

Now rape and seduction occur but rarely and yet are considered pollution of society. How much more so harlotry and fornication! For if we willingly permit non-marital sexual relations, this abomination will spread quickly in the community. The corruption of society will then be even greater and more widespread.

★ ★ ★

A Fellow Human Being

It is the positive duty of every person to love his fellow-man as himself, as it is written: "Love your neighbor as yourself."

Hence, we must speak kindly of our neighbor and we must be careful of his property, even as we are careful of our own property and our own dignity.

As the sages noted, "Whoever glorifies himself by humiliating another human being loses his share in the next world."

★ ★ ★

Bearing A Grudge

When a person sins against his neighbor, the aggrieved party should not hate the offender and silently nurture a grudge. Instead he should let him know his feelings and seek to rectify the wrong through honest criticism by asking: "Why did you do this to me? Why have you sinned against me?"

★ ★ ★

Shaming Another Person

"If anyone shames his fellow man in public," declared the rabbis, "he forfeits his share in the next world."

Consequently, one should be very careful not to humiliate another human being publicly, whether he is young or old.

★ ★ ★

Orphans and Widows

One ought to be especially careful about dealing with orphans and widows, since their spirits are shattered and their morale low—even if they are wealthy.

One should speak gently to them and treat them with dignity. Moreover, one must not cause them physical pain through hard work or spiritual anguish through harsh words. And one must be more zealous in protecting their estates than in caring for one's own.

★　★　★

Revenge and Forgiveness

A person should never take revenge, because in doing so he violates a negative commandment of the Torah: "You shall not take revenge or bear a grudge." It is far better for a man to be forgiving in regard to worldly matters, since these things are sheer vanity and not worthy of vengeance.

★　★　★

Body and Soul

There are two purposes to the Torah: the welfare of the soul and the welfare of the body.

The Torah strives to achieve the welfare of the soul by communicating correct beliefs to people within their intellectual capacity. The welfare of the body is achieved by proper regulation of inter-personal relationships.

This purpose is achieved in two ways: First, the Torah seeks to remove violence from society. It provides that no man can do as he sees fit or act in anarchical fashion; but he must do only the things that are for the common good. Second, the law seeks to train man in proper morals so that society run smoothly and orderly.

★　★　★

The Eight Degrees of Charity

There are eight degrees of charity—each one higher than the other.

The highest degree is to aid a poor man by giving him a gift or a loan, or by forming a partnership with him, or by providing work for him in order to make him self-supporting and without need of welfare assistance.

A lower degree of charity is one in which both donor and recipient are anonymous.

A still lower degree is when the donor knows the recipient but the recipient does not know the donor.

The fourth and lower degree is when the recipient knows the donor but the donor does not know the recipient.

A lower degree is when the donor places the alms in the hands of the recipient without being solicited.

A still lower degree is when the donor gives alms to the recipient after being solicited.

A yet lower degree is when the donor gives less than is required by the poor person, but does so willingly.

The lowest degree is when one gives grudgingly.

II

Man and Man

A Ruler Must Be Benevolent and Just

A KING SHOULD BE treated with great respect, and the heart of every citizen should be filled with awe and reverence for him. But even as Scripture accords the king great honor and insists that the populace respect him, so does Scripture command the king to be gentle and humble.

He should not be overly arrogant, but should act kindly and compassionately to lowly and great alike. He should direct his policies so as to protect the interests of the humble and the great; he should be concerned with the welfare of the least significant subject.

Moreover, when he speaks to the people, he must speak gently and he should generally conduct himself with deep humility. He must bear the burdens and complaints of the people with the solicitude of a nurse caring for a baby. Scripture has referred to him as a "shepherd"—this means that he must tend his flock and gather his lambs in his arms and take them to his bosom.

When a king sits on his throne, he must write a Torah scroll for himself, in addition to the one inherited from his ancestors. This Torah should be his guide and accompany him at all times. For example, he must take it with him when he sets off to war or when he returns from war; he must consult it when sitting in judgment, or even when he reclines to take his meals. He must never become intoxicated but should spend his days and nights studying the Torah and caring for the needs of his subjects.

★ ★ ★

A Ruler Must Be Humble and Gentle

A judge may not be arrogant or tyrannical in leading the community. He should, instead, be humble and reverent. Similarly, any public official who terrorizes the community unnecessarily for ulterior motives is to be punished.

Moreover, a leader must not behave contemptuously towards the people even if they are ignorant.

Just as a judge is charged to behave decently towards the people, so are the people expected to treat him with respect.

★ ★ ★

Human Life: Supreme Worth

When a court examines witnesses in a capital case, it must admonish them that capital cases are vastly different from civil cases. In capital cases, the witnesses are responsible for the blood of the accused and his descendants until the end of time.

For this reason, Adam was created alone to teach us that whoever destroys one human life it is as if he has destroyed an entire world; but anyone who saves a single human life it is as if he has saved an entire world.

Furthermore, all human beings are fashioned in the image of Adam, the first man, and yet no two faces are exactly alike. Therefore every man is entitled to say: "For my sake the world was created."

★ ★ ★

Ideal Ruler: Just and Merciful

A ruler, if he is a Prophet, must emulate God's attributes. If he metes out punishment, let him do so justly and moderately, not merely in order to satisfy his passions or temper. Since passions are bad human qualities, he must remain dispassionate and calm.

On occasion, he should be compassionate and merciful—not merely out of sentimentality or caprice, but because the situation requires such conduct. Conversely, there are times when he must be vengeful and angry towards people in proportion to their guilt, not for the sake of revenge *per se*, but because the guilty parties deserve it.

He may even be required to execute a person; but in such a case, he must do so without any vengeful and wrathful sentiment. He must, instead, perform his painful duty because of the criminal's guilt and for the welfare of the people.

Nevertheless, acts of compassion, mercy, pardon, and kindness should be performed by a ruler far more frequently than acts of wrath and punishment. For of all the thirteen attributes of God, only one implies Divine vengeance while the rest describe His compassion.

★   ★   ★

Civil Disobedience Is Sometimes Justified

The king has the right to levy taxes on the people for the needs of the government or the army. He also has the right to conscript men into the army and he may press into royal service animals, slaves, artisans, maidservants, and concubines, as well as public officials. He may also seize fields, vineyards, and orchards for the use of his army, and he has the right of eminent domain. Naturally, he must make proper compensation for such seizures.

Of course, it goes without saying that a king who annuls a law of the Torah or seeks to destroy the religion is not to be heeded.

Furthermore, a king who unjustly confiscates a residence or a field is a thief, and we may impound such properties from future buyers and return them to the rightful owners.

In sum, any law the king issues that discriminates against one class or favors one group against another or is prejudicial, is no law and need not be obeyed. A monarch who passes such decrees is really a robber.

★ ★ ★

How To Deal With Heretics

You ask me how to deal with the heretical sect of Karaites living in Alexandria and other parts of Egypt, in Damascus, and elsewhere in the Moslem kingdoms.

My answer is this: give them honor and respect. Try to come close to them through honest dealings. Be humble, trustful, and peaceful in your relations with them. As long as they are honorable and respectful to you, and as long as they refrain from invectives against the sages and scholars of our era and of the past, then you should reciprocate in kind.

Therefore I say that we should not hesitate to honor them, to seek their welfare, to visit their homes, to bury their dead, and console their mourners.

It is quite possible that through kindly and peaceful dealings we can lead them to repentance and a full return to our observances.

★ ★ ★

A Case of Libel

You ask me whether a scholarly cantor who has been libeled by several of his enemies ought to be removed from his post. My answer is this: any wise person should realize that we never remove a public official from his post because of mere gossip or libelous statements. This holds true if the libeled party has no enemies; all the more so when a man has enemies.

Furthermore, only if the accused cantor has publicly committed some wrongdoing may we remove him from office. Testimony alone may be sufficient to mete out punishment for his indiscretions, but it is not sufficient to remove him from public service.

If, in fact, the allegations prove to be valid, then we punish the cantor with the proper method, be it excommunication or flogging. But we do so privately lest we degrade the man and ruin his reputation permanently.

The important principle, however, is this: Anyone who slanders or libels a scholar or public official without eye-witness evidence is guilty of the crime of libel, and deserves to be excommunicated or flogged.

★ ★ ★

On Relations With Moslems

Moslems are definitely not idolaters. All traces of idolatry have been uprooted from their ranks and they are genuine and pure monotheists. If they distort the teachings of Judaism and ascribe to us incorrect beliefs, we must not resort to the same tactics and accuse them of idolatry. After all, our Holy Scriptures warned us against lying talk and deceitful speech.

The fact is that long ago the Moslems were idolaters and practiced pagan worship. But what of it? Today when they worship at their Mosques and sacred shrines, their hearts are really directed to the one true God in heaven.

★ ★ ★

On Inter-Religious Relations

The missions of Jesus and Mohammed have helped pave the way for the coming of the Messiah by improving the nature of mankind through the universal worship of God that has brought them near to His service. As the Prophet Zephaniah declared: "Then will I turn to the peoples a pure language that they may all call upon the name of the Lord to serve Him in unity."

How has this come about?

The whole world has been saturated with the teachings of the Messiah, the Torah, and the commandments. These doctrines have been spread to the farthest isles and among numerous heathen peoples who are now engaged in the various commandments of the Bible.

True, the Christians maintain that these commandments were once valid but are no longer binding on us. And it is also true that the Moslems insist that there are secret meanings to our Scriptural laws—secrets only revealed by their Messiah, Mohammed.

But I believe that when the true king Messiah rises among us and triumphs over all and is exalted and honored, then all religions will acknowledge his teachings and will return to the source of their faith and correct the errors of their Prophets and ancestors.

★ ★ ★

Converts to Judaism

My dear scholarly friend, Ovadiah, the Norman proselyte:

I received your inquiry asking whether you, as a convert to Judaism, are entitled to say in your daily prayers, "Our God and God of our Fathers."

I say to you: Indeed, you may say all of these blessings without changing the wording. You are just like any native-born Jew in this regard. My reasoning is simply this: Abraham, the Patriarch, was the one who taught monotheism to our people and showed them the true worship of God by rejecting idolatry and paganism. He was truly the finest missionary in our history; he brought many pagans into our fold. Consequently, Abraham is the father of all converts to our religion.

Therefore, you should indeed proclaim, "Our God and God of our Fathers," for Abraham is your spiritual father, and our inheritance is yours as well, since there is no racial distinction in our faith. Once you entered our ranks and joined the Jewish religion, there was absolutely no distinction between us and you in anything.

Let not your ancestry be insignificant in your eyes. Because if we trace our ancestry to Abraham, Isaac, and Jacob, then you trace yours to the Lord Himself.

★ ★ ★

The Treatment of Slaves

Legally, one may work a pagan slave rigorously. But even though the law allows such brutality, piety and prudence dictate that one should be compassionate and just and not cruel or abusive to his slave.

On the contrary: the master should feed his slave the best food and beverage. Similarly, the master must not humiliate his slave either physically or verbally. Nor may he shout at him excessively or direct his anger towards him. Rather, let the master speak gently to him; let him listen to his complaints and problems.

Cruelty and harshness are heathen virtues. But the people of Israel—descendants of Abraham—have received the Divine goodness of the Torah and are commanded by God's laws and statutes to be righteous and merciful to all creatures. Furthermore, of all the Divine attributes we are to emulate, mercy is predominant. For whoever is merciful receives mercy in return.

*   *   *

Inner Intentions and Outer Actions

One should never conduct his affairs with smooth talk and false flattery. Nor may one say one thing and mean another. A man's inner intentions must correspond to his outer actions; his mouth must express his inner thoughts.

It is also prohibited to deceive anyone, Jew or Gentile. We may not sell adulterated products or misrepresent merchandise. Nor may we feign hospitality or generosity when we know in advance that the person will refuse our offers.

Such actions are deceptive and false. And we are to avoid the slightest word of sham or fraud or deception. Rather, our goal should be truthful words and pure intentions and a character free of the taint of evil and corruption.

*   *   *

Charity and Compassion

We must observe the commandment to give charity more than any other commandment, because charity is characteristic of a righteous man. The glory of Israel and survival of the true faith depend on charity, and Israel will be redeemed only through charity.

Nobody ever becomes poor from giving charity nor is anyone injured because of charitable activities. If a person is cruel and lacking in compassion, we suspect his lineage, for the heathens are cruel. But Israel's outstanding trait is compassion.

He who motivates others to give charity receives an extra reward, more than the donor himself. Charity collectors and similar communal workers are even more meritorious. Daniel says of them: "Those who turn many to righteousness are like the stars."

★ ★ ★

On Evil in the World

You must remember what we have already proved, namely, so-called evils are really evil in relation to a certain thing. And that which appears to be evil is in reality the absence of some condition or of one of its beneficial aspects. Consequently, it has been stated as a general proposition that "evils are really negations." For example, death is evil for a human being; it is the absence of life. Similarly, sickness or poverty or ignorance are evil for man; they represent the absence of positive elements.

In view of this introductory statement, it must be obvious that God cannot be described as the source of evil or that his primary intention is to do evil. This is impossible: for all of His works are absolutely good. He merely creates existence and since all existence is good, it follows that evils are the absence of various qualities that are not active forces in life.

The various evils that men inflict on other men stem from evil intentions, lust, perverted opinions, or misguided religious beliefs. In a sense, they all originate in the absence of some good conditions—they all stem from ignorance, and ignorance is really the absence of wisdom. It is analogous to a blind person who, for lack of sight, constantly stumbles, injuring himself and his fellow man as well. In the same way, various classes of men—depending on the extent of their ignorance—bring various evils upon themselves and others. Wisdom is to man as the power of sight to the eye. When man has wisdom, he ceases injuring himself and others. For hatred and enmity will depart through the knowledge of truth and man will cease injuring his fellow man.

Frequently, men believe that the amount of evil in this world outweighs the good; that evil is the norm and good the exception. This error is due to the fact that such an ignorant man and his peers judge the whole universe by examining the plight of one man.

The foolish person believes that the entire universe exists for him—as if there is no other reality. When adversity strikes, he concludes that the universe is evil. If he would but examine the entire universe, he would realize that he is but a tiny part of it and the truth would be known to him. It is advantageous for man to know his true worth and not think erroneously that the world exists for him alone but is the result of the will of the Creator. Man's existence is, nevertheless, a great good and a sign of the Lord's grace in that he is uniquely fashioned. But he must realize that most of the evils that afflict men are due to themselves—that is, the flaws and defects in men.

In my opinion, there are three kinds of evil that befall men: First, there is the evil that is inherent in man's imperfect nature. Since he is flesh and blood, he is subject to various imperfections, and some people inevitably suffer from serious illnesses and deformities. That is the nature of the human constitution.

The second class of evils is that which men bring upon each other, for example, when people use force against others. These kinds of evil are even more numerous than the first but are not the most common class.

The third class of evils is the most common. It comprises evils which men bring upon themselves and it is about these evils that most people complain. This category of evils originates in human vices, namely, lust for food, drink, and sex. For overindulgence in these appetites leads to death, illness, and spiritual and physical afflictions.

When we find that evil befalls a pious man, it is because he has neglected to reflect on God and to seek to know Him. For no evil can befall a man who constantly walks with God. If man walks with God and fills his mind with Divine thoughts, it is impossible for evils to afflict him, for he is with God and God is with him. But when a person ceases to meditate on God and separates himself from the Lord, then God separates Himself from him, and such a man is exposed to any evil which might befall him.

For the intellectual glow that unites man and God is what insures Divine providence and averts evil happenings. To be sure, sometimes a righteous man suffers and an evil man prospers. But that is mere chance and not God's will. Clearly, we ourselves are the cause of God's hiding His face and we are the ones who draw a curtain between man and God. By doing so, we expose ourselves to chance and abandon ourselves to destruction like cattle. But the man who does not separate from God and causes Him to dwell in his heart, will never come to grief.

★　★　★

Law and an Orderly Society

In view of the enormous differences in individuals caused by the varied nature of men, life in society would be quite impossible without a leader who is capable of coordinating their actions, correcting their shortcomings, diminishing excesses, and laying down standards of behavior binding on all.

Thus natural differences will be submerged beneath the

accepted norms and standards—and the community will be well-ordered. For this reason, I say that the Torah, while not a product of nature, is nevertheless closely interwoven with nature.

It is part of God's wisdom to maintain the human race (since He willed its existence) by endowing the nature of certain men with leadership ability. Some persons, like Prophets and lawgivers, are therefore inspired with legislative ability; others—such as kings—possess the knack of enforcing these laws and know the art of compelling people to act accordingly.

The sole purpose of certain laws is the establishment of a well-ordered society that is free of corruption and violence. Such laws are free of philosophical speculation and have no concern for man's rational faculty or the development of human opinions, be they correct or faulty. These man-made laws are solely designed to develop a well-ordered society in which a man's relations to his fellow man are properly regulated, and they thus afford people a degree of happiness.

★　★　★

Peace Is Better Than War

One must never wage war with anyone in the world without first attempting peaceful negotiations. This applies to both optional and obligatory wars, as the Torah says: "When you approach a town to attack it, you shall first offer it terms of peace." If the inhabitants accept a peaceful solution and agree to abide by the seven laws given to Noah, then one may not kill a single resident.

Moreover, it is forbidden to break a treaty or lie to the people or betray them once they have agreed to peace terms.

If any army besieges a city to capture it, it must not surround

50

it on all four sides but only on three. The fourth side must be kept open so that the civilian population may flee and save their lives. Nor may the attacking army cut down the fruit trees in the vicinity or cut off the water supply, or destroy civilian property or homes or food supplies.

★ ★ ★

Conscription, Exemption and Waging War

Certain men are exempt from the military draft. The newlywed, the man who has recently planted a vineyard or built a new house, and the faint-hearted and cowardly. But these men who are exempt from combat are nevertheless required to serve as non-combatants: they must bring water and food to the troops and they must repair the roads.

Once a man is in the thick of battle, however, he must trust in the Lord to save him. He must realize that he is fighting for the unity of God; he must take his life in his hands and must not be fearful or terrorized.

He should not think of his wife or children but must wipe their memories from his mind so as to devote himself totally to war. Moreover, since the blood of all Israel is on his head, if he fails to do battle with all his heart and soul in order to triumph, it is as if he has shed the blood of all the people.

★ ★ ★

Peace in the Messianic Era

Do not suppose that in the days of the Messiah any of the laws of nature will cease to exist or that new creations will come into being. In fact, the world will continue as it normally does, with the one exception that Israel and her neighbors will coexist in peace and the wild, predatory nations will no longer behave like wolves.

51

All of the fantastic visions of the Prophets concerning the messianic era are metaphorical. As the sages have noted, "The only difference between this world and the days of the Messiah is that in messianic times no nation will subjugate another."

The sages and Prophets did not long for the messianic era in order to dominate the world or rule over the pagans or be exalted over them. Nor did they yearn for an era of wild eating and drinking and revelry. Rather, they yearned for the leisure and peace to study Torah and wisdom with no one to oppress them or forbid their study.

In that era there will be an end to famine and war, envy and strife. Goodness will prevail, and prosperity will abound; the universal occupation will be to know the Lord.

III

Man and God

God Is the First Being

THE FUNDAMENTAL PRINCIPLE and the pillar of all knowledge is to know that there is a First Being who brings everything into being, and everything in the heavens and on earth derives from His existence.

Nothing can exist without this Being and everything depends on Him; for this Being can exist without the creatures of the universe but they cannot exist without Him.

This Being is the God of the universe, the Lord of the entire world. He controls the galaxy with a power that knows neither end nor limit nor interruption. Since the spheres revolve and since it is impossible for something to revolve without someone causing it to revolve, it follows that God is the source of that movement. And He does so without a hand or a body.

★　★　★

The Unifying Force

Just as a man dies if his heart stops beating even for an instant so would the universe perish if the spheres were to come to a standstill. A living creature is *one* through the action of his heart—even though he has varied limbs and appendages which lack motion and sensation.

The same is true of the universe: although it includes many bodies that lack motion and life, it is still a single, living force, analogous to the heart of an animated creature. You must therefore consider the universe as one creature, endowed with life, motion, and a soul. This analogy is helpful in understanding the idea of the unity of God and that the One has created a unified universe.

It is impossible for any organs of the human body to exist by themselves and yet be an organic part of the body. Similarly, it is impossible for one part of the universe to exist without the other parts, for all are interdependent. Now just as there is a force in man that unites the organs of his body, nourishing and sustaining and protecting them (what the physicians call the "vital force in a living body," or as they sometimes describe it, "nature"), so, too, there is a unifying force in the world that protects and preserves the components.

There also exists in this universe a force that controls everything — that sets in motion all the chief components and gives them the power to move all other parts. Let no man assume that the universe can proceed without that force; for its absence would mean the end of the galaxy and the cessation of all primary and secondary functions. I call this force in the universe — God, blessed be His name!

★ ★ ★

"The Life of the World"

Everything that occurs in this world is attributable to God. Even if there are more approximate causes, He is the ultimate cause of everything. Moreover, He is the cause of all natural forms that come into existence and cease to exist, for each must be preceded by some other form in order to come to its present form. If we go back to the very inception of all forms, we find the basic form without which no other form can exist. And that is God.

Now when I say that God is the ultimate form of the

universe, you must not imagine that His relationship to the world is like that of form to matter in a physical sense. What I mean to say is this: Just as every existing thing possesses a form, without which it ceases to exist, so is God the form of the remote principles of the universe.

His existence makes it possible for everything else to exist, and He enables everything to exist by the process of "emanation." Should He, so to speak, cease to exist, then all reality including the intervening and the remotest principles would also cease to exist. Consequently, God's relation to the world is like that of form to matter, because form is what gives matter reality and true essence.

In this sense, we can describe God as the ultimate form—the "form of forms"—the being who gives existence and permanence to every form in the world. In Hebrew usage, therefore, we call Him "The Life of the World."

★ ★ ★

The Difference Between God and Man

I have indicated that metaphysics is a difficult and subtle discipline that cannot be taught to the masses. But do not think that this caveat includes teachings concerning the incorporeality of God and that He is unaffected by external causes. On the contrary: Just as we must teach the masses and children that God is one and that no other deity besides Him is to be worshipped, so must we teach the people with authoritative tradition that God is incorporeal, that He is not at all comparable to any of His creatures, that His existence is unique to Him alone, that His life does not resemble the lives of His creations, that His wisdom is unlike that of man, and that the difference between God and His creatures is not one of degree but of kind.

When the Bible or Prophets use expressions that seem to imply that God has human forms and attributes, it is merely allegorical language and is intended to help ordinary people conceive of God in terms that are meaningful to them. Such expressions, naturally, must not be taken literally, for "the Torah speaks the language of men."

I therefore am convinced that no man can doubt the truth of the idea that the Creator needs nothing for His continued existence nor does He require any improvement in His essence. Consequently, He has no organs, He is not a corporeal being, His actions are accomplished by His essence, not by any organs, and His actions, knowledge, and will are not dependent on attributes separate from His essence.

★ ★ ★

Suffering and the Jewish People

Ever since the time of Revelation, every tyrant or despotic king has sought to destroy our Torah and abolish our faith by force or by the sword. Amalek, Sisra, Sennacherib, Nebuchadnezzar, Titus, Hadrian, and others of their ilk, have attempted to wipe out Judaism forcibly. This is the first of two types of enemies who sought to triumph over Divine will.

The second category of enemies consists of the most educated and enlightened nations, such as the Syrians, the Persians, and the Greeks. They also sought to destroy our religion by arguments, debates, and polemics. Just as our enemies who resorted to force attempted to abolish Judaism, so did these enemies endeavor through more subtle means to obliterate our faith. But neither will succeed because God has promised us that we will not perish and we will outlive all our enemies. They will be destroyed, but the Jewish people will live on.

★ ★ ★

God's Negative Attributes

Let me say a few words about God's attributes. It is obvious that existence is an accident that affects all things that exist; it is consequently an added element to the essence of that matter. But in the case of a being that lacks any cause for its existence—namely, God, whose existence is absolute— its existence is its essence and character; its essence and existence are one.

He is not substance to which existence is added accidentally; His existence is absolute and perpetual, not because of any new element or accident added to Him. God exists without possessing the attribute of existence; He lives without the attribute of life; He knows without the attribute of knowledge; He is omnipotent without the attribute of omnipotence; He is omniscient without the attribute of wisdom. All combine in one entity so that no plurality can be ascribed to God.

Whenever you find God described in Scripture as "the first" or "the last," remember that these are metaphors like "God's ear" or "God's eyes." For such expressions concerning God are merely human phrases, common among men. Similarly, we refer to God as "one" in order to stress the fact that He is unique and that nothing can compare to Him. We are not, of course, implying that the attribute of oneness is added to His essence.

In my opinion the negative attributes of God are the true ones; they imply no incorrect notions or deficiencies in reference to God while positive attributes imply polytheism and imperfection in God. Moreover, positive attributes—even if unspecific—indicate some part of the thing they are describing for us. This may be either part of its substance or accident. On the other hand, negative attributes never describe anything about the essence of the object, about which we are inquiring, except incidentally.

After this introduction, let me state that it is proven that God exists by necessity and that He is not a composite. We can only conceive of His existence—not His essence. Moreover, it is false to say that He has positive attributes because that would imply He has existence added to His essence. We can only apply negative attributes to God.

Thus, when we speak of the unity of God we negate the possibility of more than one God. The point that I have tried to make is this: Every attribute describing God describes His actions, not His essence, or else is a negation of an attribute He does not have.

In view of all of the previous material, we must understand that our knowledge of God is limited. We can understand that He exists and is unique and unlike anything else in creation; that He is no plurality and is not powerless to create other beings; that His relation to the world is similar to that of a captain to his ship (even this is merely a simile to teach God's management of the world), and that He supports and preserves the order of the universe.

*   *   *

Prayer and Flattery

I cannot approve of the practice of certain fools who are extravagant in praising God and who compose endless and verbose hymns of praise in order to come close to Him. They describe Him in terms, which if applied to a human being, would suggest some imperfection.

Such people are obviously ignorant of the great and weighty matters of theology which are not available to people of ordinary intelligence. These individuals treat the Creator as if He were a figure of speech to be described in any idiom that suits their fancy. They praise Him eloquently and believe that they can thereby influence Him to their will.

There are also poets and composers and preachers who take the same license. Such compositions are pure heresy, not to mention folly and absurdity, and they surely evoke laughter and possibly sorrow in those who are amazed that such things are said about God.

If slander and libel are great sins, how much greater is the sin of those who speak loosely of God and ascribe to Him inferior attributes. In my judgment such people are not guilty of rebellion; they are guilty of profanity and blasphemy. And this applies both to those who listen to these words as well as those who utter them.

★ ★ ★

Worship—For Man's Benefit

If you maintain that all creations exist for man's benefit and that man's purpose is merely to worship God, then we have a problem. What purpose is there in man's worship of God? Surely, man does not thereby improve on God's perfection, even if everyone worships and perceives Him to the utmost degree! Nor can man diminish God's perfection by failing to worship Him!

You must, therefore, hold the view that our worship perfects *ourselves*—and not God. And why are we here on earth in possession of this potential for perfection? The answer is that we are here on earth because God willed it so and His wisdom has decreed it to be so.

★ ★ ★

The Reasons for Ritual

The masses of scholars believe that there is a reason for every ritual, that there is a purpose to every commandment. Of course, we sometimes fail to perceive the rationale because of our limited mental and intellectual capacities. But every commandment has some useful purpose.

What are the purposes of the commandments? There are several—and this applies to both positive and negative precepts.

The commandments are designed to remove injustice, to teach proper morals that help improve society, and to convey true beliefs which we should acknowledge either on their own merits or because they help remove injustice and promote proper morals.

Doubtless you know from the numerous passages in the Bible that the primary purpose of the Torah is to uproot idolatry and to wipe out every trace of it. Consequently, we are warned against magic and necromancy, witchcraft and augury, sorcery and human sacrifice, seances and black magic. We are not to imitate any of these loathsome and abominable practices nor may we ever adopt them.

Similarly, we may not shave the corners of our head and beard because this was the practice of idolatrous priests. Nor may we wear combinations of woolen and linen garments or mix different species or graft diverse types of trees because this was a common idolatrous practice connected with pagan rites and licentious orgies. In order to sever all connections with such idolatrous abominations, these rules were instituted.

But there are other reasons for the ritual laws.

The rules that required us to give offerings to the Temple, the Priests, the Levites and the poor were obviously designed to instill in us a feeling of pity for the poor and the weak so that we would assist those in need and avoid hurting the unfortunates of society, like the orphans and widows. Such laws were instituted in order to implant in our hearts the quality of generosity and to diminish our lust for food and passion for wealth.

Another reason for ritual is the social value that ritual serves. For example, the purpose of the festivals is clearly evident. Man benefits from public assemblies, his religious loyalties are renewed through such activities. Moreover, he develops a love for his co-religionist and a love for the group to which he belongs.

Of course, many laws are designed to curb excessive lust and animal drives so as to raise man to a higher level of perfection and induce him to live according to the golden mean.

In sum, the ultimate purpose of the laws of the Bible is to revere God, to fill our hearts with knowledge of Him, and to love Him. Love comes through the doctrines of the Bible— including the true knowledge of God's existence. Reverence is nurtured by observing the practices of the Law.

★ ★ ★

On Reading the Bible

Some of the narrative portions of the Bible contain deep wisdom not immediately apparent to the reader. Consequently, many people fail to comprehend the deeper meaning. Some people actually see no value to those portions—as, for example, the passages listing the descendants of Noah and other such sections.

Know well that every story of the Bible serves some vital function. Either it seeks to verify one of the fundamental beliefs of the faith or it is designed to regulate human actions so as to remove injustice and violence between human beings.

For example, the detailed genealogies given in the Bible (Genesis 5 and 10) are designed to instruct us in the cornerstones of the faith—namely, that the universe was created by God out of nothing and that we are all descendants of one, single ancestor, Adam.

As another illustration, let me cite the story of Abraham and the war of the kings. That tale serves several purposes. It shows the power of a miracle that enabled Abraham to defeat four great kings, with a handful of men and lacking a military chieftain. Moreover, the story informs us of Abraham's compassion—for his concern for his kinsman Lot moved him to risk his life in war in order to redeem him from captivity. Finally, the episode instructs us as to the contented nature of Abraham. For he was a man who coveted no material things but was content with his portion in life; he scorned wealth and gloried in moral excellence. And the proof is that after he won the battle with the four kings, he refused to take any booty, "not even a shoe lace."

In sum, remember that in reading the Bible, you must reckon with the fact that there is often a hidden level not immediately apparent to the eye. If you fail to perceive the inner truth, the failure is apt to be yours—not the Bible's.

* * *

Sabbath: A Double Blessing

God has commanded us to abstain from work and to rest on the Sabbath for two reasons.

First, by doing so we affirm the true belief in the creation of the universe. This belief leads us immediately and unequivocally to a belief in God's existence.

Second, the Sabbath reminds us of God's mercies over us. After all, He freed us from the slavery and oppression of Egypt and gave us a day of rest.

The Sabbath is, therefore, a double blessing for us: It implants correct notions in our minds and it promotes our physical welfare.

★　★　★

Science and God

Let me open this chapter with a parable.

A king is in his castle; some of his subjects are in the city, some are outside of it. Of those in the city, some have their backs turned to the palace and their faces are towards another direction. Others want to make their way to the royal palace and are anxious for an audience with the king. But hitherto they have never seen even the walls of the palace.

Some visitors have succeeded in finding the palace but not the gate; others have discovered the gates and have entered the forecourts; and still others have succeeded in entering the royal chambers but have not yet been granted an audience with the king. Further effort is still required to actually see and speak with the king.

Now let me explain this parable that I have invented.

The people outside of the capital city are the masses who have no religious faith whatever, whether it be speculative or traditional. Such people are sub-humans; they are lower than men, but higher than apes.

Those people who dwell in the city but whose backs are towards the king are the men of false speculation and incorrect opinions. They are worse than the first kind.

The great mass of people consists of those who seek to enter the palace but cannot find it. Such people are those who obey the commandments but are not very learned.

Those who have arrived at the palace but circle it in a vain search for the entrance are the people who possess religious learning and proper beliefs and observe the traditions and keep the practices of the faith serving God. But they are deficient in speculating on truth or investigating the principles of the faith.

But those who have immersed themselves in speculation on the principles of religion have entered the forecourt; they have found proof for that which can be proved and have penetrated the Divine truths (as far as such truths can be discovered) and have actually approached the presence of the king in his royal chambers.

Therefore, as long as you study mathematics and logic you are like those who wander in search of the gate. Once you study natural science, you enter the forecourt of the palace. And after completing your study of natural science, and if you master metaphysics, then you enter the king's inner chamber and you are at one with him. This is the highest level of the learned—though there are different degrees of perfection.

★ ★ ★

Superstition and Religion

We are not permitted to engage in witchcraft as do the pagans. For example, the person who refuses to go to a certain place out of fear of bad luck because a piece of bread fell from his mouth or a stick slipped from his hand, is a foolish, superstitious individual.

So is the man who refuses to leave his home because a fox crossed his path on the right side. And people who derive recondite meanings from the chirping of birds, or who set store by specific signs or happenings, are sinning and deserve to be flogged.

★ ★ ★

Astrology, Charms, Seances

It is forbidden to engage in astrology, to utilize charms, to whisper incantations over wounds, or to communicate with the dead in a seance. In fact, a sorcerer deserves to be stoned to death if he engages in witchcraft.

All of these practices are nothing more than lies and deceptions used by the ancient pagan peoples to deceive the masses and lead them astray. It is unseemly for the people of Israel, an intelligent and enlightened people, to follow such foolish and absurd practices and to believe that there is some use to this nonsense.

Indeed, anyone who believes that there is some scientific validity to these superstitious practices is really a fool and an ignoramus. Wise and intelligent people know better.

★ ★ ★

Two Ways to Emulate God

There are two ways in which a man can imitate God and walk the middle road.

First, a man can train himself in these moral traits until they become part of him. He can practice these traits time and again until he develops temperate dispositions. Ultimately, they will be simple to perform; they will cease being a burden and will be ingrained in his character. Since these ethical attributes are associated with the Creator, they constitute the middle path we are required to follow, the path called "the way of the Lord."

The second way to cultivate Godly character traits is by proper associations. Man's natural instinct is to think and act like his friends and colleagues and emulate his peers. Therefore, a person should constantly associate with righteous people and wise men so that he might learn from their example.

And he should shun evil men who walk in darkness lest he learn from their ways. This is what King Solomon meant when he wrote: "He who walks with wise men becomes wise, but he who befriends fools will suffer."

★　★　★

The Knowledge of God

Only those who cultivate both religious practices and mathematics, logic, natural science, and metaphysics are privileged to enter the inner courtyard of God. Only after having thus comprehended Him and His works—according to the degree of man's intellect—can man devote himself to God and strive to come near to Him and strengthen the bond that links man to Him—namely, human intellect.

Love of God is proportionate to the degree of knowledge.

Service of God—such as worship—follows after love.

In my view true service to God consists of exercising one's power of thinking with regard to God, the Primary Intellect, and in concentrating as far as possible on Him. Clearly, the aim of man in life is complete devotion to God and the perpetual exercising of intellectual thought in order to love Him.

The possessions men seek with such fervor and which they consider the highest perfection are really not the height of perfection; nor are the religious practices of the Torah and worship, nor are moral virtues regulating inter-personal relationships the highest perfection in man.

None of these can compare to the highest goal and ultimate purpose in life—namely, the knowledge of God.

★   ★   ★

God in Man's Daily Life

A man should direct his mind and heart and all of his actions exclusively towards knowing God. Whether he is sitting or standing or talking—everything must be directed towards that goal.

How? For example, when one engages in business, his purpose should not be merely to acquire wealth. Instead, his purpose should be the acquisition of enough money to provide for bodily needs—food, drink, shelter, and matrimony. Similarly, when a person eats or drinks or copulates, his goal must not be mere pleasure; rather he should eat or drink in order to strengthen and heal his body and limbs. He must, therefore, not eat like a dog or a donkey and select merely the sweet foods that tickle the palate. Instead, let him eat foods that are salutary for the body—even if they are distasteful.

Likewise, when one copulates let it be for health reasons and in order to propagate the species. A man should not, therefore, engage in sexual relations whenever he desires. Instead, let him do so when his health requires the release of sperm, or in order to bring children into the world.

★ ★ ★

The Middle Course

The right way of life that man should follow is the middle road of character traits and dispositions, that is, dispositions that avoid the two extremes.

How does one do so?

A person must not be hot-tempered or phlegmatic, but of medium temperament. He should be angered when an important issue is at stake, and anger is justified as the only means of preventing a repetition of an injustice. Likewise, he should desire only those things necessary for the body and for life, as it is written, "The righteous man only eats enough to satisfy his needs."

He should engage in enough business to satisfy his daily needs. He should be neither tightfisted nor overly lavish but should offer charity according to his means and extend loans to those in need. A man should not be lightheaded nor frivolous, nor should he be solemn or mournful. But he should be joyful all of his days; his countenance and disposition should be cheerful. This principle also applies to other traits. And this is the way of the wise. He who avoids extremes and follows the middle path in life, he is truly a wise man.

★ ★ ★

Pride and Anger

Sometimes a person should not choose the middle course in cultivating specific traits. For example, one should utterly shun the sin of pride by going to the opposite extreme. The right way is not to be merely meek, but to be of lowly spirit and exceedingly humble.

Similarly, anger is a terribly evil disposition and a person must shun it by cultivating the opposite extreme. He must teach himself never to lose his temper even when a grave issue is at stake that rightly demands anger.

When a man strays from the middle path and moves to an evil extreme, the only cure is to spend a long time at the opposite extreme in order to find the middle path once again. For example, if one is haughty, the only cure for him is to spend time in abject humility, so as to rectify his spirit. Then he will return to the middle course, which is truly the good one.

★ ★ ★

Man: Master of His Fate

Man is the master of his fate and free will is given to us all. If a person chooses to do good and be a saint, the power is in his hands; if he chooses to do evil and be a wicked person, the choice is his. This is what the Bible meant when it declared: "Behold man has become like one of us, to know good and evil."

Do not, therefore, delude yourself with the nonsense spread by fools that states that the Holy One preordains from birth whether a man will be righteous or wicked. This is sheer nonsense: Every man can be as righteous as Moses or as wicked as Jeroboam—wise or foolish, merciful or cruel, stingy or magnanimous—or have any other quality of character he chooses.

And no one can compel him to act a certain way; no one can predestine him to follow a particular path; but he himself has the power to choose whichever path he would follow. That is what Scripture implied by stating: "Evil does not proceed from Heaven."

For if God decreed whether man is to be a saint or a sinner, or if man were innately destined to follow a particular path of morality or develop a certain disposition or character or perform various deeds—as the ignorant astrologers claim—then how could the Prophets command us to act this way and not act another? How could they admonish us to mend our ways and avoid the path of evil?

If man is predestined to do good or evil, how can he ever hope to avert his fate? If pre-destination were a fact, what role would the Torah serve?

Do not be astonished at what I have said. And do not wonder that man can do whatever he wishes in view of our belief that nothing happens in this world without God's will. Know well that we all do God's will, but He wants us to have free will and the option of acting as we see fit.

★ ★ ★

Free Will

Man is born without any innate merit or corruption. True, it is possible that he is born with certain dispositions based on biological factors. But, normally, man's actions are entierly up to him, for nothing can compel him to act the way he does, since free will is given to man. This must be so or else we arrive at an absurd position.

72

For example, if Simeon killed Reuben, how can you hold Simeon guilty since he was predestined to kill Reuben and Reuben was predestined to be killed? Indeed, if a person acts criminally due to compulsions beyond his control, we cannot hold him morally or criminally responsible nor can we punish a criminal.

Consequently, we must accept without doubt the belief that man's actions are determined by his own free will: if he wants to do something, he does it; if not, then he abstains from doing it. And no force can compel him to do so. He is, therefore, a responsible creature. He can perform God's will—or violate it, as he chooses. As the sages have noted: "Everything is in the hands of Heaven except the fear of Heaven."

★   ★   ★

Man Can Change His Character

Once we accept this view of man's nature, namely, that he acts out of his own free will in choosing good or evil, we understand why we must teach man the difference between the good or the evil way of life.

We must command him to do good; we must warn him against corruption; we must punish his rebelliousness; we must reward his virtue.

This is the equitable way to run society. Likewise, a man must accustom himself to virtuous deeds until they become part of his character. And he must abstain from sinful acts until he sheds his natural depravities. He must never say: "I cannot change my ways and improve." For a man can change his character from good to evil or from evil to good. Everything depends on his free choice and will.

When does man lose his free will? Only when God punishes him for his sinfulness by depriving him of his free will.

★　★　★

Moral Virtues Come First

It is clear that moral virtues are prerequisites of intellectual virtues. The attainment of true intellectual values, that is, perfect intellectual conceptions, is impossible except for the man who is morally trained, calm, and stable.

The man of sensuality and lust, of levity and rashness, and of excitable disposition can never achieve intellectual perfection.

In order to study philosophy, a man must prepare himself morally; he must first achieve the pinnacle of uprightness and perfection.

Sources

MAN AND HIMSELF

The Difference	*Guide for the Perplexed* I, 35 and 46
Suffering	*Letter to Yemen*
God's Negative Attributes	*Guide for the Perplexed* I, 57 and 58
Prayer	*Guide for the Perplexed* I, 59
Worship	*Guide for the Perplexed* III, 13
Ritual	*Guide for the Perplexed* III, 26–50
On Reading the Bible	*Guide for the Perplexed* III, 50
Sabbath	*Guide for the Perplexed* II, 31
Science	*Guide for the Perplexed* III, 51
Superstition	*Mishneh Torah, Avodah Zarah* XI, 4, 6, 7, 8
Astrology	*Mishneh Torah, Avodah Zarah* XI, 12–16
Two Ways	*Mishneh Torah, Deot* I, 6 and 7; VI, 1
Knowledge of God	*Guide for the Perplexed* III, 51 and 54
God in Daily Life	*Mishneh Torah, Deot* III, 2
The Middle Course	*Mishneh Torah, Deot* I, 4
Pride and Anger	*Mishneh Torah, Deot* II, 2 and 3
Man and Fate	*Mishneh Torah, Teshuvah* V, 1–4
Free Will	Introduction to *Pirke Avot*, VIII
Man Can Change	Introduction to *Pirke Avot*, VIII
Moral Virtues	*Guide for the Perplexed* I, 34